The 7
Deadly Sins

That Are Crippling Your Business... And
The 3 Step System For Attracting And
Converting Your IDEAL CLIENTS...

John Mulry, MSc

John Mulry, Msc

What others are saying about
John Mulry...

"John was lucky enough to be personally mentored and trained by me. As a GKIC Certified Business Advisor, he's equipped with an arsenal of tools that any small business owner can pick up and run with to start producing big time, bottom line results. This is exactly the kind of advice I needed when I started my career... but nobody who really knew what was going on was willing to share. If you're a business owner and you want real improvement in your business then I highly suggest you listen to what John has to say."
– Dan Kennedy, Dan Kennedy, Serial Entrepreneur, Multi Millionaire and Highest Paid Direct Response Marketer in the World

"The thing about John that most people aren't willing to do, is to actually apply the best practices that they learn to their own business and life in order to achieve maximum effectiveness in minimum time." **- Nick Nanton, CEO of the Dicks Nanton Celebrity Branding® Agency, Emmy Award Winning Director, Producer & Best-Selling Author**

"If someone had told me you will get an extra €10k in your bank account from doing this [working with John], I would have laughed but yes this has transformed my business and the results were outstanding. I closed a total of 24 clients once I activated what I had learned. It totally changed by way of

thinking and how to approach my marketing strategy. The results were immediate. Get on board and get the information."
- John T Kenny

"Right from the very first interaction I had with John, which was getting his book "Truth About Marketing" all the way to someone to one consultation time, I have been blown away by the actionable advice I have received. Even if I implement just a few things he suggested, it will add €1,000's to my income over the coming months and years. He's one of the most knowledgeable and sincere marketers around." - **Gareth Sherry**

It didn't take long for John's marketing gems to click on a few light bulbs for me and set me straight, as I put together my new advertising campaigns. Yep, light bulbs is a good metaphor - I feel as if a whole series of darkened mind corridors have been illuminated and revealed! But that's not all. John was so generous in contacting me personally to sort out some tech issues, a great reflection of his generosity in sharing his expertise and giving value to so many."
- **Doreen Mellor**

-

"Working with John, he helped me develop some simple but very effective sales and marketing strategies that have helped me close sales and increase revenue for my business. John's in depth knowledge of marketing and his easy to apply systems are a huge benefit to any business needing a boost. Highly recommended." - **Don Neachtain**

"Surpassed my expectations so much that I am in awe (I have never used that word in m life). One of the most helpful contacts I have ever had with any marketing consultant and I have years of personal experience with consultants - a few in the excellent category, so I am not just comparing him to the usual ones but to the best."

- **Lee Parratt**

John Mulry, Msc

ISBN-13: 978-0-9928003-4-5

7 Deadly Sins is available at special quantity discounts for bulk purchases, for sales promotions, premiums, fundraising, and educational use. For more information, please write to the below address.

Published by: Expect Success Academy
Unit 14, Ballybane Enterprise Centre
Galway, Ireland

www.JohnMulry.com

First Edition, 2016

Edited by: Jessica Thompson - www.Jessica.ie

Cover Art by: Sam and Bax

Published in Ireland

To you, the business coach, consultant and/or marketer...

You're out there helping businesses do more, be more, help more and get more. You deserve your own accolades, your own success and your own recognition. Thank you for everything you do. Remember: EXPECT SUCCESS...

In life, you don't necessarily get what you want and you don't necessarily get what you need. Instead, you get what you honestly and truly believe you deserve. In other words, you get what you expect, so why not EXPECT SUCCESS?

–John Mulry

Table of Contents

Preface – Why This Book?

Before we dive deep into the 7 DEADLY SINS in this book I first want to set the stage by doing a few things:

1. Share a little of my own story so you can understand where I'm coming from.
2. Outline why it is you're not getting the results you think you should be getting.
3. Introduce you to the Expect Success Cycle.

Once we've covered those three areas then I will walk you step by step through the seven deadly sins that are crippling your business.

And I don't say crippling your business lightly. These sins, on their own are dangerous but together they ARE downright deadly to your marketing business, your consultancy business and/or your coaching business.

Your ability to find, attract, convert and keep clients is severely hampered by any or all of these sins and it is my goal to at the very least help you be more aware of them so you can stop them, thwart them and do everything you can to overcome them so you can attract, convert your most IDEAL clients.

Clients who appreciate you, clients who pay you what you deserve – clients you'll love doing business with.

Let's begin with a simple question…

Why?

Why do you do what you do?

Why are you in business?

Are you doing things just for money or do you have stronger reason? What's your reason why? As we're going through this book have that question in the back of your mind.

On the topic of why, there are four reasons why I've written this book for you:

- I'm sick and tired of people NOT succeeding.
- If you have read or will read my first book *Your Elephant's Under Threat,* you'll know (or will discover) that my creed, my mantra, my everything in business is…INVEST, CONSUME and ACT…

- I have a big mission of instilling the INVEST, CONSUME and ACT into the lives of 1 million people before 2030 and to achieve it, I'm going to need your help.
- Writing this book allows me to attract potential partners who will be able to help me achieve my mission and profit from it at the same time. I'll be talking about this a little later on in the book.

Before we dive in I quickly want to introduce myself personally to anyone who may be new to me, my business, my way of doing things or maybe you need a little refresher into who the hell I am anyway.

I hate talking about myself so I'll keep it as short as possible so we can get into the juicy stuff.

My background is originally in Corporate Finance, I (luckily and quickly figured out I hated the corporate world and quit everything in 2009 in the middle of the recession and went volunteering in South America for a year where I got to work with some amazing people and have some amazing adventures.

While I was in South America I realised that I loved helping people and when I came home a year later I began working on starting my own fitness business.

This all came about via a lifetime of low self esteem, bullying, failure after failure, borderline alcoholism a year long trip of volunteering in South America, swimming with sharks, being rescued by helicopter, ending up in jail (wrongly) in Brazil and whole lot of massive action and change.

The full story of all of this is in first my book *Your Elephant's Under Threat*.

When I started my fitness business, I quickly realised two things:

1.   If I couldn't market my business I'd fail and
2.   I was more interested in the marketing behind my business than the fitness.

I then discovered that I was not only more passionate about marketing; I was actually a hell of a lot better at it than most.

That's when the 'Maverick' started to sprout.

I started reading and studying marketing, I became so engrossed in marketing and advertising both online and offline that found out that I was actually very good at it, so good that it made me realise that it was my true passion.

I immersed myself in the world of direct response marketing, I started buying books, courses and attended events in London, Birmingham, Manchester, California and Texas.

That conference in Texas set the wheels in motion. Little did I know that conference would introduce me to someone called Dan Kennedy in a much bigger way than I thought possible and become a twist of fate that changed my life forever...

I ended up being handpicked and trained by my marketing mentor Dan Kennedy and GKIC to become their main guy in Ireland which completely changed my business and my life. I've authored four books (apart from this one), have contributed to three other books and have three more books in the pipeline.

I currently live in Galway with my girlfriend Jess and my dogs Sam and Baxter. Like I mentioned my mission is to help 1 million people by 2030 and I'm passionate about people who invest in themselves…

My work, my books, and training programs have been endorsed by some of the top marketers and business minds in the world like Dan Kennedy, Brian Tracy, Tom Hopkins, Clate Mask of Infusionsoft, Nick Nanton to name a few and I tell you this not to impress you but to impress upon you, if I can do this SO CAN YOU…

Because…

I'm giving you the exact framework you need to succeed in this book and I'm even going to show you how to fast track that success if you want it…

Who This Book is For...

This book is for business coaches, business consultants, marketing consultants, agencies and offline marketers but not for all of them.

This book is specifically for those who meet the following six criteria:

1. You have honest ambition.
2. You're frustrated and disillusioned with not attracting the type of clients who value you, pay you what you're worth and appreciate you.
3. You have a strong study ethic (you read books, study the best and constantly strive to improve)
4. You have strong work ethic (you don't expect everything to be handed on a plate)
5. You have the capability to implement what I will show you.
6. You're in business to help people first and profit second.

If you fit these six criteria then congratulations – you're a special breed of coach, consultant and marketer and you'll love what I have for you in this book.

Why You're Not Succeeding...

To succeed in business whether as a coach, consultant, marketer or any business for that matter there's certain things you need to do but before you succeed you need to FIRST understand why you're not succeeding... here's the truth about running an coaching, marketing and/or consulting business.

Some of this may hurt but you need to hear it. Trust me you'll thank me afterwards.

- There are lots of shiny objects out there, lots of people trying to sell you things, some are genuine, and sadly most are not. This confuses you meaning you're not sure what to focus on.
- You got into this with the goal of making money for yourself and your family but maybe you're disillusioned because you keep spending money and not making it. This may seem like something small but it's one of the keys to you succeeding and I'll explain why in a moment.
- Sales letters and Guru's make it sound so easy... they're filled with promise and give you hope – so you buy even though they might not be right for you at this moment in time but you

get sucked in anyways just in case this new report, software or gizmo might contain the magic ingredient you're missing.

- You buy the product/course/software and no actionable content – and more often than not, what you were promised was not what you got. In fact what you got was a rehashed thing you had already – no magic ingredient here. Or worse you don't even go through it.
- Then you move onto the next shiny object and buy again.
- And the cycle continues and you continue to jump from one thing to the next to the next – I'll explain why this is now...

All of this starts from within you in the first place because you have what's called a flawed mindset or brainset. I talk about this in depth in my first book *Your Elephant's Under Threat* but let me quickly explain this to you so you can once and for all break the cycle.

The focus of the flawed mindset and brainset is on:

- Shortcuts
- Quick fixes
- Easy ways out
- 'Magic' solutions

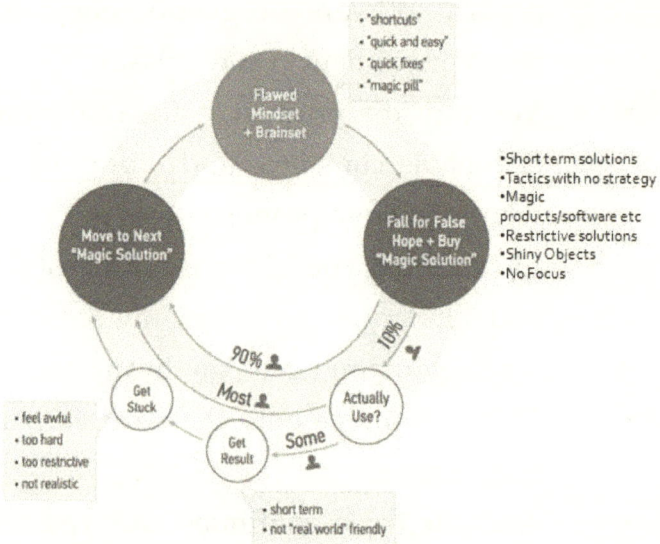

- "shortcuts"
- "quick and easy"
- "quick fixes"
- "magic pill"

Flawed Mindset + Brainset

- Short term solutions
- Tactics with no strategy
- Magic products/software etc
- Restrictive solutions
- Shiny Objects
- No Focus

Fall for False Hope + Buy "Magic Solution"

Move to Next "Magic Solution"

90% 👤

10% ✓

Most 👤

Some 👤

Get Stuck

Actually Use?

Get Result

- feel awful
- too hard
- too restrictive
- not realistic

- short term
- not "real world" friendly

You're always on the lookout for a shortcut to success, a quick fix, an overnight, push-button, done-for-you solution. These are the quick fix, magic bullet solutions and promises of overnight success. For example, in your business you fall for a hyped up solution that promises to boost sales by 1000% without spending any money or doing any work.

Or in terms of health, the magic exercises, pills, powders, and lotions, or the secret berry from the Amazon Jungle that melts fat. Or the magic pill that guarantees to turn you into a fitness model with no dieting or exercise.

Obviously these examples are a little exaggerated, but you get the point. The next stage of the short-term cycle comes for you after you fall for the hype. You fall for the hype and the hoopla and buy the "magic product" in the hope that it'll end your woe and give you everything you want.

Now after you buy into the shortcuts, quick fixes, and easy-way-out solutions, 90% of the time you don't even use them. You do nothing. If it's a book, it sits on your shelf or on your hard drive.

You never read it, consume it, or apply it. Same goes for software, or a piece of equipment, or a pill, powder, or potion. 90% of the time they don't get used.

Whether that's down to you not having time or deep down not fully trusting it to give it proper time and focus, I'm not sure.

You start to feel angry, even more frustrated, alone, and depressed, but lo and behold, another bright and shiny object comes your way. The cycle continues.

Now, out of the 10% that actually use the "quick fix solutions," you might achieve some results, but chances are they are going to be short-lived. You'll get some results. You might even make a bit of money (if it's business-related), you'll feel a bit better... but what you're doing isn't long-term.

It isn't sustainable, and when a roadblock comes along, you won't be able to deal with it. The first sign of frustration or feeling stuck and you'll end up right back at the start, falling for the next magic solution or shiny object.

Because what you were doing was too hard, too confusing, too embarrassing, too restrictive, sometimes even illegal, or not fit for the "real world" or for real people with real lives and real commitments.

Does this make sense?

The sooner you realise that the above cycle is seriously flawed, the sooner you can go on to actually start achieving your goals.

Take a second to think about whether or not you're in or have been in a cycle similar to the short-term flawed cycle. It can be completely draining, depressing, and expensive, can't it?

When you start to gravitate towards the long-term cycle, you'll forget about the shiny objects very quickly and the flawed mindset/brainset cycle becomes a distant memory.

Do you want to know how to fix this once and for all?

The Expect Success Cycle

MAKE DECISION

TAKE ACTION

DO SOMETHING

THOUGHT

INPUT

EXPECT SUCCESS CYCLE

SUCCESS

I want to introduce you to the expect success cycle. In order to change, you've got to do something, simple as that.

To do something, you have to take action. To take action, you've got to make the decision to take action.

And of course, any time we make decisions, these decisions are manifested from our thoughts.

So here's the Expect Success Cycle in its simplest form: your thoughts lead to your decisions, your decisions lead to your actions, the right actions lead you to doing something worthwhile, something worthwhile leads to success.

It's a simple cycle that works.

There's one fundamental problem. Our thoughts are managed by our input. When the wrong input influences your thoughts, the decision, action, do something cycle is completely ruined – absolutely ruined.

Generally speaking, we get our input from news (online or offline), gossip, politics, friends, family, peers, staff, co-workers, partners, competitors, etc. Now, when it comes to news, gossip, and politics, that's nearly always negative input.

The messages we get from them are usually that the world is ruined, you can't trust anyone, and people are inherently bad. Our other sources of input like friends, family, partners, staff, etc. can also provide negative input (some more than others), which drives home even more negative messages.

Now, with that being the input, how do you think that's going to influence your thoughts? If all the input you're getting is danger, people are bad, etc., what decisions will you make in life? Think about it. Every minute you're making a decision.

Will I read this book? Will I finish it? Will I change? Will I take action? Will I go to work on what I'll learn?

Millions of decisions are being made by your subconscious and conscious mind every day. Remember, your subconscious is the majority part of your mind and thinking capability. So when you've got the news (with all that danger input) on in the background and you think you're not listening, it's entering your subconscious mind and your subconscious controls your thoughts and your decision-making, which leads to your actions, which leads you to making a half-hearted attempt at doing something.

What happens is your thought process will lead you to make the wrong decisions, you'll take the wrong action and make a half-hearted attempt at something, you divert to not doing the right thing, which leads to no success, or failure.

Why? To support the beliefs that are being instilled by all of your negative influences. Are you starting to see how all these roadblocks are connected to your ability to change? The actions we take have to be congruent with the input we get to support our beliefs.

When your input is correctly aligned with your core values, your Expect Success Cycle is complete. You don't pay attention to the noise, nonsense, and negative input variables, and you only listen to what's going to bring you forward – that's when you start to realise that the sky's the limit.

This will become a lot clearer if we were ever to work together and when you discover your core values. You'll start to see more clearly how and why we need to keep tabs on these roadblocks.

Does this make sense?

Now at this stage you might be thinking what the hell does this have to do with you attracting and converting more highly qualified coaching and/or consulting clients?

Well the short answer is EVERYTHING.

If you focus on the wrong things and your INPUT is all negative and of the short term mentality then how the hell you are going to make the right decisions and take the right action needed to start attracting your most IDEAL clients.

You can't. That's why the expect success cycle is so important.

And now you understand it it's time to go through each and every one of the *7 Deadly Sins That Are Crippling Your Business...*

The 7 Deadly Sins That Are Crippling Your Business...

7 Deadly Sins? Sounds like something out of a movie right? Well it's not; these deadly sins are specifically related to your business and if you're even just making one of them you're missing out on lost leads, clients and sales. I'm going to go through each Sin – explain why it's a sin, it' implications and what you can do to stop it dead in its tracks.

Once we've covered all seven sins I'm then going to give you my three step system for attracting, converting and keeping your ideal clients again and again. Ready? Let's go.

John Mulry, Msc

Deadly Sin #1: Not Knowing Who THEY Are...

Deadly Sin #1:
Not Knowing Who They Are...

Who is your most IDEAL client?

Sadly this is a question that often times we think we know the answer to but rarely do. The first deadly sin that most coaches, consultants and agencies are making is not clearly defining EXACTLY who they want to serve and just as important who they do NOT want to serve.

When you know exactly who you're for and who you're not for you get distinct advantages over your competitors.

For one – you get to narrow your focus to a particular niche or industry and you can actually afford to spend more to acquire a customer and he (or she) who can afford to spend the most to acquire a customer - wins.

Secondly, when you're unsure of who your most ideal clients are its very easy to get pulled left and right by clients you don't like working with, by clients that annoy you (it happens right?) and into projects and "opportunities" that suck you of your time, resources and your money.

How do you go about choosing your ideal clients?

And I don't say choosing lightly, you should be engineering your business to work with the exact clients YOU want to work with, after all – it's your business right?

It's always helpful if you have an affinity with the type of clients you want to work with. For example if you were in the fitness industry and you're now a business coach you might look at targeting personal trainers or gym owners as you can relate to them and you know the industry.

In saying that, when you decide who you want to work with you must ensure that your IDEAL clients fulfill the following three attributes:

1.   A need or desire you cater to.
2.   Care about getting an answer to that need or desire.
3.   Be able to pay your price for that answer.

There's absolutely no point targeting people who have no desire for what it is you offer, or worse they can't pay your price for that answer.

When you settle on your ideal client, don't waste your time or resources pitching to any other kind of prospect. You want to focus on finding, attracting and converting only those who are in your target audience while similarly driving others (who are not in your target audience) as quickly and as cheaply as possible.

Remember:

<u>Be very clear and up-front about who you ARE FOR and who you AREN'T FOR</u>

Who is your most IDEAL client?

Start with some of your existing clients or if you're new outline who you would like to work with the most. Keep in mind the three attributes they must fulfill:

_____

_____

_____

_____

_____

_____

_____

_____

Deadly Sin #2: Not Thinking Like Them

Deadly Sin #2:
Not Thinking Like Them

Deadly Sin #2 could be the key difference between you getting clients and you not getting clients, between you thriving or starving.

One mistake all business owners make is that they don't often enough (or ever) put themselves in the shoes of their ideal customers.

Essentially they don't think like them or speak their language.

This chapter is going to be a mini lesson in copywriting, a mini lesson in the art of attracting clients by what you say, and how you say it and the language you use.

One of the biggest reasons you're not attracting the clients you know you could be attracting is because you're not thinking like them.

To move someone, to compel them and to convince them you must first think like them and then you must speak their language, not your own.

Too many coaches, consultants and agencies fill their marketing and advertising with jargon and platitudes that your target market neither care about nor understand.

For example if you're a digital marketing agency you're focusing on things like website optimization, search engine optimization, social media marketing, content marketing and things like that when the bottom line what your target market wants is...

RESULTS!

You should be focusing on the RESULTS that your strategies or tactics bring them.

Your clients and potential clients want more leads, more customers, more referrals, and more profits.

And these are all problems that your potential clients have and need solving. Switch your focus to providing SOLUTIONS to those problems and start using their language.

Everything you do should be in their eyes and written for them because when they look at your marketing or advertising or when they speak to you they are thinking

"What's in this for me?"

Make sure you're giving yourself every opportunity to answer that question as much as you can – think solutions to THEIR problems.

Remember:

Your clients don't care about HOW you get them RESULTS as long as you get them RESULTS.

Take what you're currently offering in terms of your products of services. How do they relate to the problems your target market have and how do they SOLVE those problems?

_____
_____
_____
_____
_____
_____
_____

Deadly Sin #3: Not 'Making Sales To Get Customers'

Deadly Sin #3:
Not 'Making Sales To Get Customers'

Here's the key to a long and profitable business:

You don't get a customer to make sales; you make a sale to get customers.

Re-read that sentence so it sinks in, there's a subtle difference in the wording of both phrases but a world of difference in the implications and results of each.

The majority of businesses are focused solely on making sales, and forget the fact that in order to make sales you need to get a customer.

The true power and leverage in your business is when you shift and start making sales to get a customer.

Here's what I mean.

A buyer is a buyer is a buyer, just like a tyre kicker is a tyre kicker and will always be a tyre kicker. You want to focus on attracting buyers in your business and the best way to do that is to make a sale to get a customer.

Instead of going out there and offering your high end coaching off the bat or going straight to offering your $15K - $20K website or program or whatever you should first offer something of value to your target audience that turns them from a lead to a buyer. And then once they are a buyer you ascend them up your ladder of ascension.

For example, imagine you had your own book – now I'll be talking about this a little later on in more detail but imagine for a second that instead of offering your high end offers straight off the bat (which is very hard to sell to new leads) you instead offered them your book (for example they cover shipping and handling and you sent it to them for free) they have now become a BUYER and you made a (albeit small) sale to get a customer.

Having a BUYER is way more beneficial than having lots of leads.

Adding more value to that buyer a.k.a. helping solve more of their problems will lead to more sales and more sales. If your book was geared around helping them make better decisions as it relates to your product or service –

who do you think they are going to choose to work with – the person who helped them or the person constantly selling to them?

Making sales to ACQUIRE customers allows you to build an audience of buyers whom you can add value to again and again.

Best of all this is a rinse and repeat process. The art of this having multiple widgets in the marketplace is one that can turn leads into customers quickly and is one of the best ways to start attracting the right types of clients for your higher priced offers.

So how can you do this?

Well for example if you're offering high end business coaching... that costs say $997+ a month. Trying to sell that to cold leads will be very difficult. Not saying it can't be done but it won't be easy.

Instead if you splintered out one or two elements from your high end coaching and packaged that up into a product, course, book or tool to sell in the marketplace you'd be attracting qualified BUYERS instead of 'looky loo' tyre kickers.

For example imagine for a second that you help business owners maximize the productivity and efficiency of their staff. No easy task but let's imagine for a second that this is your specialty.

Instead of offering your $10,000 package you offered had a book or a course on staff productivity that you sold for say $7 - $197 (depending on the actual type of offer).

When you market and advertise that and position it correctly (which I'll be talking about later) – anyone who buys it is now a customer and your job is to add more value to them and obviously the highest value YOU can offer someone is your personal expertise a.k.a. your $10k productivity program.

Is this starting to sink in?

When you realise this – everything becomes a whole lot easier and it becomes a numbers game. A certain percentage of people who opt for your widget will also opt for your high end offer.

And by offering your widgets up front (making a sale to get a customer) you're actively building your heard of buyers. This is where the magic is. Having your own herd or tribe as its sometimes known is a fantastic position to be in.

Anytime you release a new widget, a new course or a new product you can offer it to your herd and if it adds value to them and makes their life easier, better or allows them to achieve their goals faster a certain percentage will buy it.

Why? Because they are buyers. This is the beauty of shifting your business from: getting customers to make sales to: Making a sale to GET A CUSTOMER...

Remember:

<u>A buyer is a buyer is a buyer is a buyer... all day long!</u>

What kind of splintered from your high end offers can you package up and sell to your target audience? Think in terms of elements you can take or slice off your higher priced offers that you can easily package up and profit from again and again. Think in terms of books, courses, products, online tools, resources etc.

_____

_____

_____

_____

_____

_____

Deadly Sin #4: Not Charging What Your Worth

Deadly Sin #4:
Not Charging What Your Worth

Deadly Sin #4 is something that all businesses fall into. Not charging what you're truly worth. How often have you undercharged for your products or services? How often have you've been afraid to charge what you're worth in fear that you would lose the sale? How often have you instantly discounted your products/services as soon as you state your prices to prospective clients – just because there was an uncomfortable silence and just in case they say no?

I remember the first time I learned about pricing and learned about stating price. It was actually BEFORE I even started my first business. Like I mentioned in the letter that got you to get this book in the first place, I'm a little strange.

Strange in that BEFORE I even stared my first business I was knee deep in all different types' of business books trying to get ahead and trying learn as much as possible.

I guess it was my natural passion of advertising and marketing (that I didn't really know I had at the time) that made me gravitate towards books on these topics. There was one book in particular that I was listening to over and over again while in the gym.

Yes, in case you're not aware, actually listening to books is a great way to expand and continuously learn more and more if you're not a fan of reading or don't have time.

I am fan of reading but enjoy listening to books also.

Anyway, the book I was listening to was called:

'How to master the art of selling' by Tom Hopkins. Tom is a legend in the field of sales and I highly recommend this book.

One of the points in the book which really stood out for me is what to do after you've named your price.

He said: 'Once you name your price, SHUT UP and don't say another word until they say something.' Great advice. Too often we can instantly start discounting our prices and offers even before our prospects had a chance to say anything.

Have you ever done this?

So yes, not charging what you're worth is another DEADLY SIN.

So in order to start charging what you're worth you must understand and be crystal clear on exactly HOW MUCH YOU ARE WORTH.

Do you know how much you are worth?

How much you're time is worth?

Not how much you're time is worth currently because let's face it, chances are you're woefully under pricing yourself, how much your time would be worth if you were getting what you should be getting on an hourly or daily basis.

Now I don't recommend you pricing your services or your products on a per hourly basis. Your business and your pricing should be priced in accordance to the value you are bringing to your target audience.

If I were to price my partner program at $20,000 you might say that's a lot but if I said it has the capacity to bring you in $100,000 per year + recurring commissions from product sales then that $20,000 doesn't seem so expensive now right?

It's not anywhere near $20k by the way…

Have you constructed a very small box and locked yourself in it? Here are five ways you can overcome the deadly sin of not charging what you're worth…

5 Ways to Start Charging What You're Worth:

#1: Don't agree to be a commodity. Be and offer something special, extraordinary, fun, with a great story attached.

#2: Don't sell in a competitive environment. Create a "category of one" by some means so there is no apples-to-apples comparison possible -- radically different pricing, furnished turn-key promotions, contests, bundled goods and services.

For example, I've created a category of one by offering a Done-For-You lead generation, attraction and conversion system for consultants, coaches and/or agencies through my partner program. More on this later.

#3: Think "Place Strategy". Where is the place, distribution or sales opportunity no other providers are exploiting?

Examples: the jewelry store set up at racehorse auctions, the luxury mattress store set up at classic car auctions, sell and ship direct to consumers.

#4: One way to flip an ordinary commodity into a different, more interesting, more valuable product is as a gift item.

#5: If you want a great lesson in making the ordinary and mundane seem revolutionary and fascinating, take a couple days off and watch home shopping, QVC and HSN.

The success of most businesses overtime is derived...

- 50% from the ability to consistently acquire a sufficient quantity of valuable customers.
- 50% from the ability to keep those customers interested.

Thus the need to frequently re-purpose, re-imagine, create, present something new, the next big, interesting idea, story, person, thing.

You can find it driving most exceptionally successful businesses. If you let your business drift far from this 50/50 balance, in either direction, your ship may crash on the rocks.

Which of these five areas do you need to strengthen?

_____

_____

_____

_____

_____

_____

_____

_____

_____

_____

_____

John Mulry, Msc

Deadly Sin #5: Not Using Systems

Deadly Sin #5:
Not Using Systems

This sin is something I see a lot of coaches, consultants and/or agencies making time and time again. Not using systems in your business in this day and age really is criminal, yet it is still common place.

What do I mean by using systems?

Simple, I mean marketing systems and marketing automation.

When it comes to marketing and advertising – the majority of businesses, not just coaches, consultants and/or agencies plan to generate leads and close sales usually falls down to dumb luck. In that, they have no plan and no system for attracting, converting and keeping clients.

Any marketing they do have is of the 'one and done' variety.

Instead you should employ systems in your business, multi-step, multi-media systems where you put in the hard work to build them once and then reap the benefits of them over and over again.

I'll be walking you through some specific examples of the best type of systems to use in your business in a later chapter but think of things like this.

What can you do in your business to engineer leads and sales coming to your business automatically?

For me there are six critical systems you should have in operation in your business:

1. Lead Generation System(s)
2. Lead Nurturing System(s)
3. Automatic Selling System(s)
4. Continuity Income System(s)
5. Referral System(s)
6. Lost Customer Reactivation System(s)

Bear in mind that these systems are not limited to one medium – they can and should combine both online and offline elements together.

Take the process on how you got this book.

You seen an ad (either online or offline) were sent to a landing page and were offered this book (something of value to YOU – which I'll discuss next by the way).

Then there was a follow up system to send you this book and there is a subsequent campaign to invite you to apply for one of my partner programs.

The whole process is a series of systems linked together through the power of multi-step multi-media marketing combined with marketing automation using various software's, suppliers and vendors.

Sounds like work and it is – but once its setup – you can turn it on and off when you like, generate leads and sales when you like.

This is a VERY POWERFUL position to be in.

Remember:

The key to a profitable, repeatable and scalable business is SYSTEMS.

Which of the six systems is the most pressing for you to build?

_____
_____
_____
_____
_____
_____
_____
_____

Deadly Sin #6: Not Being an Information Marketer

Deadly Sin #6:
Not Being an Information Marketer

If you're a coach, consultant, agency and/or offline marketer and you're not consistently and STRATEGICALLY adding value to and educating your clients you are seriously missing out on a lot of untapped revenue and profits.

Adding value to your target clients doesn't mean giving away free content until your blue in the face nor does it mean blogging every hour in the day.

STRATGEICALLY adding value to your target audience is imply the act of being pre-eminent. You go above and beyond to help your target audience with a problem they might be having ahead of asking for anything in return.

This can come in the form of blogging but it can and should be much more than that.

The best way to strategically add value and educate your target audience is through INFORMATION MARKETING.

Here's the big secret...

You may want to grab a highlighter or heck put this in a big BOLD type at say 100pt font size and stick somewhere in your office, practice or home where you'll see it every single day...

People will come to you faster and stay longer to learn something (of value to them) then they will ever come to you to be sold to.

That's the secret right there... those 27 words hold the key...re-read that sentence again so it sinks in.

When it comes to the application of the marketing strategies

I've walked you through the bottom line is this...

To get the best results possible, instead of advertising your business, advertise SOMETHING OF VALUE to your target audience...

When you do this you cross the threshold and become an information marketer...

And no matter what your business is – being an information marketer is a VERY good marketer to be...

Why? Well for starters here are three reasons:

1. Materials perceived as information are better received and given more attention than materials perceived as just advertising.
2. Salespeople have sales literature. Trusted advisors have information.
3. Advertising free or nearly free, useful information is a low-threshold offer.

Typical advertising and marketing that doesn't offer anything of value but merely advertises the business is only attracting a very small percentage of people in your target audience. High threshold offers like a visit with a salesman a test drive or dental exam are useful but solely using them means you're missing out on and deterring a large proportion of people who would otherwise be interested in what you have to offer.

Here's what I mean...

This is something the late great Chet Holmes popularized years ago but sadly it's been forgotten with the rise of the fancy and distracting new gadgets, gizmos and shiny objects in online marketing and media.

The problem with 95% of ads and marketing materials out is that they are trying to sell from the page.

Marketing and advertising is like dating...

To get the best results when it comes to dating you cannot just walk up to a complete stranger you've never met before in a bar, nightclub, coffee shop gathering, event or wherever and say

"Hey, I think we should get married, have three kids, two dogs and a cat." – At best you'll get laughed at, at worst you'll get a slap or a drink thrown in your face...

It's the exact same scenario in business ... why oh why do we think it's okay to go out and try and get married on the first date?

That's what selling from the page is...

Have a look at ads online, in magazines, newspapers and on the radio, the majority are trying to jump straight to marriage and kids...

Sure you can pick up some customers this way but when you sell from the page generally what's happening is you're attracting customers who shop based on price and you're only attracting now buyers...

At any given moment no matter what it is your business is selling out of your target audience there is only 3% who are actively looking for what it is you sell...

Only 3%... that's it.

And this doesn't mean 3% of whoever sees your ad – it means 3% of your target market who see your ad.

That's a big distinction.

After the 3% of people actively looking to buy next up comes 7% of people who are open to what it is you have to sell. These are people who aren't in buying mode but are on the lookout.

Even combining those together is only 10% of your potential market.

What about the other 90%? Well:
- 30% of these are open to it but are NOT ACTIVELY thinking about it...
- 30% THINK they're not interested and finally
- 30% are definitely not interested...

When you understand this dynamic everything changes… these figures aren't made up… these are based on empirical evidence from more than 200 industries and on aver-age these are the figures…

And the best way to start tapping into the other 90% or at least 60% f it is by using some informational offers that are either free or low cost.

What are some examples of informational offers?

1. Useful information that educates your target audience on how to make better decisions as it relates to your product/service industry.

For example – a free or low cost book (like this one).

2. Useful information on HOW TO BUY

This could be a booklet or DVD, CD on things your potential customers must know before they do business with you (or anyone).

For example:

11 Things You Must Know About Health Clinics, Weight Loss Clinics and Weight Loss Specialists BEFORE You Purchase.

If your target audience is people looking to lose weight – what's going to work better – advertising your business or advertising a FREE booklet, video, DVD or CD on the X things they must know before buying.

This is so simple is genius.

Here's a template you can use no matter your business or your industry.

_____ Things You Must Know About _____, _____ and _____ Before You Purchase.

Here are some examples:

•   The 7 things every business owner should know about websites, social media and marketing online before ever spending a penny.

•   The 9 things parents should know about entrepreneur should know about staffing recruitment and hiring the right talent before they hire staff again.

- The 7 things every marketing consultant, business consultant or coach needs to know before they go after high paying clients.

As you can see these are not complicated.

Other variations of this are:

- Everything you ever wanted to know about before buying _____ but were afraid to ask.

- The Consumer's Guide to _____ and _____

- The buyers Guide to _____

This type of informational offer that shoes people how to buy is so valuable to them and to you it makes you the only logical choice when it comes to making a decision.

Like I said it's so simple its genius.

You're simply taking the knowledge you already have and you're packaging it up in a way that your target market will want.

That's what information marketing is all about.

And best of all, you do the work once and you can use it again and again and again.

I get very excited about this stuff.

It's not in the slight bit complicated – and when you've this finished you've something that will generate leads for you night and day.

You can offer it on your website, hand out printed copies, have offers for it on your business cards, and create ads offering it in newspapers, magazines online on Facebook, Twitter etc.

When people request it they telling you:

1. They're in your target audience
2. They need and want a solution to a problem
3. They're ready to buy

Can you understand the power in this?

And best of all it's not rocket science – you could put this together in a few days.

Do the work once and profit from it again and again.

It will become your biggest marketing asset and will transform your business.

Deadly Sin #7: Not Using the A.C.E. Formula

Deadly Sin #7:
Not Using the A.C.E. Formula

The last deadly sin (in this series – I'm already planning a second edition) is one that if you fix – holds the key to fixing all previous six too.

The 7th Deadly Sin is not using the A.C.E. Formula in your business.

What is the A.C.E. formula?

Well it stands for:

- Authority
- Celebrity
- Expert

If you are not actively and consistently positioning yourself as the AUTHORITY, the CELEBRITY and the EXPERT in your marketplace then you are seriously missing out.

Frank Kern one of the most talented and charismatic marketers of our time has this to say about AUTHORITY:

"Authority – possibly one of the most influential market positions one could ever hold. Think about it, a person of authority tells us to go do something; we often unquestioningly go do it because they told us to." - Frank Kern

One of the BIGGEST reasons why many coaches, consultants and marketers fail is because they have no... **AUTHORITY.**

It doesn't matter if you have the best idea ever, if no one buys it, you're not going to make any money...

Having authority in a market, means people will listen to you...

It's the same with **CELEBRITY.**

You can and should be using the art of celebrity in your business as much as possible.

Think about it, the highest paid people on earth are celebrities right? They get paid seemingly obscene amounts of money just because of who they are and what they can do.

Now I'm not claiming you can go out there and be the next Kim Kardashian or 'The Rock' Dwayne Johnson but there's absolutely nothing stopping you from positioning yourself and strategically using celebrity in your business so your target customers see you as a celebrity.

To do so you need to have the third component of the A.C.E. formula in play: **EXPERT.**

There's an old saying: *"It's not WHAT you know, it's WHO you know."* Like most old sayings, there's an element of truth to it. But what's missing is the related truth: The more WHOs that know WHAT you know, the more money you'll make.

In other words the more people who view and see you as an expert the more leads you'll generate, the more sales you'll make, the more clients you'll convert and the more money you'll make.

The trick is to get comfortable with who you are... and who you are not.

1.	What do you do better than anybody?
2.	What do you do well?
3.	What do you do adequately?
4.	What do you do so badly, it's embarrassing?

Take the time to actually answer those four questions then put all your focus in 1 and 2 and then outsource the rest or partner with or pay other who can do them for you

So how do you become an expert?

Well you can become an expert through the following:

- Legitimate personal experience
- Read the top ten books in the field
- Read two years of industry journal back issues
- Join trade associations
- Attend a major trade show, con-vention, or conference
- Attend an industry leader's seminar
- Keep a notebook of unanswered questions - then get them answered
- Seek out several leaders in the industry and consult with them personally (informally or formally)

Becoming an expert is ONLY HALF THE BATTLE.

Arguably the more important half is being RECOGNISED as an expert. You can be recognized as an expert by the following:

- Write a book. Create information products.
- Do high profile advertising in industry journals.
- Launch a publicity campaign.
- Write articles for industry journals.
- Speak at industry conferences and/or market and conduct your own seminars.
- Publish a newsletter.
- Surround yourself with recognized experts by having them write for your newsletter, speak at your seminars, interview them for audio products, etc.

AUTHORITY, CELEBRITY and EXPERT combined equal the A.C.E. formula and there is no better strategy for attracting and converting your most ideal clients.

Out of all of the ways to become recognized as an expert there is no better than having your own book because not only does it make you the **EXPERT but it ALSO gives you MASSIVE AUTHORITY and CELEBRITY.**

WRITING A BOOK can be the fastest most powerful and profitable way to gain authority, celebrity and expertise in your niche.

Here's some of mine and trust me when I say it – these have been LIFE CHANGING for me.

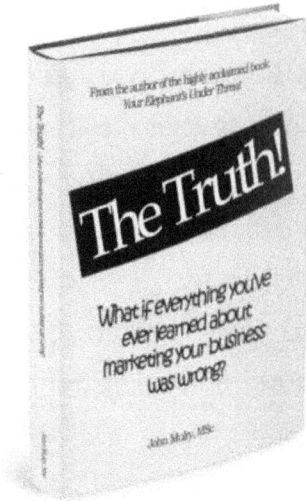

Why you should consider writing a book:

- A Book is the ULTIMATE lead generation tool…
- It positions you as an AUTHORITY, CELEBRITY and EXPERT all in one go…
- It's the BEST business card you'll ever have…
- It brings you the BEST clients…
- It's something that has TRUE value
- Remember adding value = Sales
- Make a sale to get a customer (like I discussed earlier)
- List of Buyers created – you go from lead generation to buyer generation…

Remember:

There's no quicker, faster and more enjoyable way to attract and convert clients than doing so with authority, celebrity and expert status.

What ideas have you for a book?

What could you write about that positions you as the authority, the celebrity and the expert in your marketplace?

_____

_____

_____

_____

_____

_____

_____

_____

_____

_____

_____

_____

_____

Problems, Process and Positioning...

Problems, Process and Positioning...

Now that we've discussed the 7 deadly sins that are crippling your business – it's time to map out the THREE STEP system for attracting, converting and keeping your most ideal clients.

Some of these points have been touched upon as I walked you through the 7 deadly sins and you may have picked up some of them if you've been paying attention.

In fact the three step system actually ensures you don't fall victim to any of the 7 deadly sins that are crippling your business.

My simple three step process consists of:

Step1: Problems
Step 2: Process
Step 3: Positioning

Let's start with Step 1 – Problems.

You need to focus on your client's problems NOT yours.

Forget about what you have to offer. Forget about what it is you do. Focus on what YOU CAN DO FOR THEM. Remember it's about THEIR DESIRES not yours.

If you make the focus of your marketing and advertising around establishing what their pain points are, what their problems are then actively engineering your business in a way that OVERCOMES or solves their problems you're on a winner.

How do you establish their pain and find out what their problems are?

Well the easiest way is to ask them, ask your existing clients, speak to people in your target audience, speak to them online in forums and in person.

Here's another strategy that you can use to get boatloads of market research done for you for free.

Go to Amazon and start searching for items related to your niche whether it's books, products etc.

In the search results filter by the most popular and the ones with the most reviews.

Read the reviews (both good, bad and ugly) – the feedback here is from paying customers (most of the time) they happily tell you what they've loved, tell you what they hated and even tell you what they wish was included or what was missing.

Amazon from a research point of view can be an absolute goldmine and it will help you outline exactly what your target audience problems are.

Also another way you can start to think like your target audience and find out what their pain and problems are is by putting yourself in THEIR SHOES and answer the following questions.

If I could just _____?

What is that is keeping them up at night staring at the ceiling? What do they secretly, ARDENTLY desire? Once you know what that pain is, what that problem is, it's your job to find the solution. And then you offer them the solution. It's as simple as that.

Remember:

Stop talking in terms of what you do but WHAT YOU CAN DO FOR SOMEONE.

What is your target audience's #1 problem?

_____

_____

_____

_____

_____

_____

Once you know their problem or problem the next step is process.

Step #2: Process

Like I mentioned with Deadly Sin #5 - You need to have a system and process for putting people through that qualifies and converts them.

Remember these words: repeatable, profitable, and scalable. That's what processes or systems allow you to achieve in your business.

You need a process for putting your prospects through that gets them to put their hands up and say, *"Hey, I'm interested in what you have to offer..."* and then that system should qualify and close them also.

Here's an example of six step system you should look at incorporating into your own business:

Step 1: Lead Generation
Step 2: Qualification
Step 3: Diagnostic Advice
Step 4: Prescription
Step 5: Deliver and Wow
Step 6: Referral Generation

You should pay attention each step because each is as important as the previous but pay specific attention to the words: Qualification, Diagnostic Advice, Prescription, and Wow.

It's fairly easy to generate leads these days with the multitude of options available both online and offline and especially if you're actively using information marketing and advertising something of value to your target audience.

But the key is generating QUALIFIED leads.

No use in generating leads that are unqualified. I can't tell you the thousands I've wasted in generating unqualified leads. Now I put the majority of my time and focus on generating only the most qualified of leads.

Once those leads are qualified then next step is to diagnose and prescribe.

Remember you're the authority, the celebrity and the expert and this gives you the privilege to diagnose and prescribe just like any other expert.

You diagnose by asking diagnostic questions that get to the root of what your ideal clients are looking for help with and then and only then do you prescribe an action plan.

And your close – well your close becomes easy…

It's simply six words:

Would you like help with that?

Having the right process in your business will afford you a freedom you can't imagine and the final piece of the puzzle is by adding in the power of positioning.

Step #3: Positioning.

Positioning is arguably the most important part of the whole process because you can find out your target audiences problems you can have a process but if you're positioning is off you won't be able to prescribe and you won't be able to command pricing and fees you deserve and you won't be able to stand out in your crowded marketplace.

The right positioning allows you to be seen as the trusted advisor instead of a salesman and rightfully so, you have the ability to change your ideal clients lives and the right positioning allows you to become THEIR trusted advisor.

Like I've mentioned the fastest and easy way to gain the ultimate positioning that gives you authority, celebrity status and positions you as the expert is with your own book.

This three step process is the exact process I've used in my own business to attract high quality, highly qualified leads, sales and customers and I suggest you not only read these words but you put them into action and implement this three step process into your own business.

John Mulry, Msc

The A.C.E. Formula Revisited

The A.C.E. Formula Revisited

Most GURUS' don't want you to know about the A.C.E. formula let alone you actually implement it.

They want you to stay confused so they can sell you more stuff.

They want you to view them as the Authority, them as the Celebrity and them as the Expert.

And rightfully so, a lot of them are authorities, celebrities and experts – but that doesn't mean that you can't be either.

How can you start this? How can you start writing that book that will position you using the A.C.E. formula?

Take an hour a day, every day, and invest it in one thing: writing, or creating publicity to become an EXPERT in something. You'll be "world class" in that very fast.

One hour a day of truly, totally con-centrated effort can equal most peoples' 8 hour workday.

Now if you're thinking...

"But I'm not an authority... I'm not a celebrity and I'm not an expert... I can't compete with the big GURU's..."

You're probably right, you can't compete with them but you DON'T have to...

Just a little more knowledge than the rest can produce exceptional leverage.

Here's one of my favourite quotes by Desiderius Erasmus:

"In the land of the blind, the one-eyed man is king."

You don't need to know everything, you don't need to know as much or be as big as the GURU's you just need to know more than your target audience knows and make sure what you know can add value to them and make their lives easier, faster or better.

Like I mentioned writing a book on a topic close to your business and close to your core offer, products or services will become the ULTIMATE lead generation tool for your business. It positions you as an AUTHORITY, CELEBRITY and EXPERT all in one go..., it'll be the BEST business card you'll ever have…and it'll bring you the BEST clients…

Remember Deadly Sin #3 – Not Making The Sale to Get a Customer? And remember how I said that a buyer is a buyer is a buyer?

Here's the quote again just so it sinks in:

"You don't get a customer to make sales; you make a sale to get customers"

Your new marketing system could consist of the following:

- Give your book away free or low cost using the FREE + Shipping model.
- Buyers of the book are offered a consultation
- On consultation you GENUINELY help them get closer to their goals.
- At the end of consultation you simply ask: *"Would you like my help with that"*
- You close them on your products/services.
- Rinse and Repeat…

Someone who gets your book and reads it WILL want your help…They will want to know how you can help them.

Now you offer your products/services…or your high end coaching or high end consultancy programs. This is a rinse and repeat process you can use again and again. Do the hard work once and profit from it again and again.

Now this sounds simple because well – it IS simple…

BUT

Simple ≠ Easy

Simple ≠ Easy

Simple ≠ Easy

Writing a book that positions you as an authority as a celebrity and an expert is the ultimate tool to grow your business BUT while the process of doing so is simple – it is not easy.

To help you with the process I'm going to walk you through a method to make things easier for you but first there are a few things I want to make sure you're aware of:

- This does take work…
- This does take effort…
- Writing a book while not as hard as you might think does take a LOT of work…
- Building a system to convert leads into qualified clients takes work…

In saying that – it gives you the ULTIMATE freedom…

There is a time AND money investment needed to do this but it will be money well spent.

So where do you start? How do you go about doing it? Well remember in Deadly Sin #6: Not being an Information Marketer?

That chapter on the why you need to be an information marketer holds the key.

You don't have to be a marketing guru to do this.

The best way to go about writing your book is to simply take the knowledge you already have (as it relates to helping your target audience) and you package it up in a way that your target market will want.

That's what information marketing is all about.

And best of all, you do the work once and you can use it again and again and again.

I know what you're thinking and you probably have some questions right?

What will I write about? How long will it take?

Well remember the templates I gave you earlier? These can form the basis of your book and can even become your book by fleshing them out and adding in some extra detail.

Here are the templates again:

- ____ Things You Must Know About _____, _____ and _____ Before You Purchase.
- Everything you ever wanted to know about before buying _____ but were afraid to ask.

- The Consumer's Guide to _____ and _____

- The buyers Guide to _____

Let's take this book for example:

The 7 Deadly Sins That Are Crippling Your Business and The 3 Step System For Attracting and Converting Your Ideal Clients.

I've essentially taken the template "_____ things you need to know" and changed it slightly.

You could do the same thing. Now some questions I get asked a lot when I start talking about this method are:

How many points do I use – 11, 7, 10, or what?

Use as many as you want to use, I'd say stick with a minimum of 5 but usually 7, 9, 11 or 13 are good starting points. As long as each of the points are helpful and will help your target audience improve in some area that's all that matters.

What should I talk about in the points?

Talk about things your prospects should know in order to make better decisions. This is easy, there is so much information that you take for granted that your prospects have no clue about.

Simply educate them while combining that educational material with future pacing – i.e. – getting them to imagine what their life will be like after achieving their desired result as it relates to your product or service.

How long should it be?

It should be as long as it needs to be. No longer nor shorter. Warning there's a lot of idiots out there peddling that copy be it in a video on website in a letter or anywhere should only be a certain length and that any longer and it won't be read.

Pure hogwash and those peddling that nonsense are un-educated fools.

Harsh? Possibly but the fact of the matter is that the difference between success and failure with your copy does not come down to length it comes down to **how interested they are in it and how engaging it is.**

For example, you're reading this book, if people didn't read long copy then all books would only be one page and all movies a couple of minutes.

Yet movies are 2-3 hours or more and books have a couple of hundred pages on average.

The length needs to be as long as it needs to be.

I was once asked this question and I eloquently answered it in a way that's worth repeating and definitely worth remembering:

The best copy is neither long nor short. Neither better in print or in video neither spoken nor read. The best copy, the copy that evokes a DIRECT RESPONSE is as long as it needs to be... Not a word longer or shorter...

Should I include anything else?

Yes, of course but you want to be strategic about what you include.

Here's a starter list of sections to include:
- Table of Contents
- Your Story
- About Your Business (In terms of what you CAN do for them)
- The X Things They Need to Know
- Next Steps
- Offer Specific for Readers
- Testimonials
- Frequently Asked Questions
- Questions You Wish Your Prospects Would Ask
- Contact Information
- Re State Specific Offer for Readers

See, not in the slight bit complicated – and when you've this finished you've something that will generate leads for you night and day.

You can offer it on your website, hand out printed copies, have offers for it on your business cards, and create ads offering it in newspapers, magazines online on Face-book, Twitter etc.

Essentially you'll want to build a whole marketing system around it like I talked about in the last chapter. It will become your biggest marketing asset and will transform your business.

But while this whole process is simple it's not easy and will require an investment of time and money to complete it. An investment that's well worth it mind you...

Now if you were to look at going the traditional route of writing, publishing and marketing your book and building all the systems to go with it you could be looking at the following investments of time and money:

Write a book – 100 hours+ (x $100 / hour)	$10,000+
Edit your book	$1,500+
Physical Copies say 100 copies	$500
Marketing campaign for the book	$15,000
Press Releases and Promos	$1,000
Consultant/Book Funnel Design	$10,000
Total:	**$38,000**

Now I'm not saying you have to go to that level but you could and it would be worth it.

You could even add in extra products/programs/training in your book funnel and a start an information business on the side with multiple products and even start a continuity income business if you wanted.

But obviously all of this is a LOT OF WORK and may be out of the scope of what you can do due to time and resources.

What if I could fast track this whole process for you?

What if I could hand you a **DONE-FOR-YOU** solution that positions you as the authority, celebrity and expert without any of the headaches of having to write a book, get it edited, get a cover – would you be interested?

What if I could hand you a **DONE-FOR-YOU** solution that gives you all the marketing collateral to promote your book, a marketing funnel built to help you launch it, actually provide physical copies of the book to start you, press release campaigns to get you local media attention and DONE-FOR-YOU consulting funnel for qualifying and closing your most ideal clients – would you be interested?

Well if you're interested and if you don't mind, allow me to take a few moments to introduce you to *The Ultimate A.C.E. Formula Partner Program*

And if after you think you'd like to partner with me you're more than welcome to apply.

What is The Ultimate A.C.E. Formula Partner Program?

Well before I tell you what it is I think it's important to stress what it is NOT:

- This is NOT another training program...
- This is NOT a coaching program...
- This is NOT a cheap, dated membership site...
- This is NOT a rehashed piece of PLR crap...
- This is NOT for newbie's…
- This is NOT a get rich quick scheme...
- This is NOT a magic pill...
- This is NOT cheap...

What it is...

This is a once in the lifetime opportunity to partner with me and get my exact systems, my exact marketing funnels and marketing collateral to use as your own to build your own business and get high paying long term clients.

There will be no guesswork involved.

You'll have everything you need to succeed.

You will be recognized as an authority, celebrity and expert in your area and potential clients will be actively putting their hands up to do business with you.

Here's Everything You Get With The Ultimate A.C.E. Formula Partner Program If Your Application Is Successful...

- A Strategic Partnership between you and me...
- Area Exclusive Program – no competition and no threat of saturation...
- Dedicated Territory by city or zip code (depending on location)
- A Proven-to-Work business model for generating $100k+ a year
- Done-For-You PHYSICAL Book that positions you as an expert, authority and celebrity...
- Co-Author License to one of my top selling books to use to get HIGH PAYING clients, speaking engagements, partnerships and more...
- A Done-For-You custom proven to convert four step marketing campaign...

- 100 Physical Copies of the book (with option for more at cost price) ...
- Press Release and Media Campaign and other promo tools. to kickstart your success...
- Done-For-You Business Cards and Brochure...
- Lifetime Access to Any Training Released in the future
- Ongoing Training to help ensure your success...
- Step by Step hand holding and launching of your new business over 90 days...
- Three Levels of Advisor Program to Choose From...

PLUS - Depending On Which Level You Apply and Qualify For...

- Done-For-You Book Funnel That generates Leads For You On Autopilot
- Recurring Monthly Commissions Side Information Business With A Full Suite of Information Products and Marketing Training To Sell As Your Own
- Done-For-You Consulting Funnel That Qualifies and Gets Potential Clients to Apply to Work With You...
- Custom Marketing/Sales Scripts For Videos/Presentations...

- Custom Client Procedures, Agreements and Contracts...
- Qualification Process and Diagnostic Selling Scripts.
- Tools, Resources and Training To Ensure You get Your Clients The Best Results Possible...

Obviously an opportunity like this isn't just open to anyone and everyone. There are some qualifying criteria that you would need to fulfill in order to apply.

How This Program Came About...

Now, at this stage you may be wondering, how and why this program came together and why am I inviting you to apply.

I can certainly understand your skepticism and weariness, after all there's an awful lot of tripe, snake oil and flat out scams being offered these days...both online and offline.

I'm doing this for two reasons:

1. I genuinely enjoy working with forward thinking; successful people that want to help businesses and want to increase their income by doing it.

2. There's only so much I can do ALONE.

Whereas I have the systems in my business to attract my own qualified high paying clients as I please, I have a bigger mission in life.

My mission is to help 1,000,000 people by 2030 and honestly I cannot do that alone.

My partner program enables me to help you which in turn enables you to help businesses which in turn enables them to help people and the end result is together we achieve the goal much faster than I could ever do on my own.

If you're interested in applying visit www.doneforyou.ie/partners to find out more and apply.

One thing I would like to stress is while this is a partner program in that you will be getting everything I just described you will be promoting YOUR OWN BUSINESS not mine.

We will be co-authors but the book and all the campaigns and extras that come with it will be redone to **<u>POSITION YOU as the authority, the celebrity and the expert</u>** (not me) and you will be able to offer your own coaching, your own consulting and your own high end products and services.

If you're interested in applying visit www.doneforyou.ie/partners

Your Next Steps...

Your Next Steps...

I want to thank you for one getting this book and two for ACTUALLY taking the time to read it.

Investing time and money into your own learning is one of the best investments you can make.

INVEST is the 1st rule of success to me.

By getting this book in the first place you invested in yourself and if you're reading this I can hopefully assume that you not only invested in it, you also CONSUMED the information within these pages.

The second rule of success for me is CONSUME.

One must INVEST in themselves and then they must CONSUME.

Finally the last rule of success for me is to ACT.

I want you to ACT on what you've discovered inside these pages. And that doesn't necessarily mean applying for my Ultimate A.C.E. Formula Partner Program. Sure I'd love for you to apply but at the end of the day, whether it's with me or on your own I want you to ACT.

Take action.

INVEST, CONSUME and ACT and you're well on your way to achieving whatever it is you want to achieve.

Remember:

<u>You don't necessarily get what you want and you don't necessarily get what you need, instead you get what you honestly and truly believe you deserve. In other words, you get what you expect, so why not EXPECT SUCCESS?</u>

JM

About John Mulry

"Helping entrepreneurs grow their business and profits through successful online and offline direct marketing systems."

John Mulry is an award winning and trusted marketing advisor, speaker, and top selling author with a unique, deep knowledge that spans both online and offline direct response marketing. He helps business owners get more customers, referrals and profits through his consulting, his done for you marketing funnels, his training courses, books, strategic marketing club and private business group in Galway.

When John first started his business rather than accept the status quo of the impending doom of the recession he sought out and has studied under some of the most world-renowned experts in business, direct response marketing and coaching. Experts including marketing legends Jay Abraham and Dan Kennedy, GKIC, lifestyle and business experts Tony Robbins, Dax Moy, and Emmy award winning movie director/branding agent Nick Nanton.

He lives and breeds by his creeds "invest, consume and act" and having an "expect success attitude". John was handpicked by Dan Kennedy and is Ireland's only GKIC Certified Business Advisor.

John has been featured as a guest contributor on

numerous publications including Business.com, TweakYourBiz, NUI various newspaper and publications as well as been a guest speaker for the SCCUL Enterprise Centre, OMiG, JCI Galway, Galway Chamber of Ireland, the Elite Performance Academy, All-Ireland Summit, Plato and the Ennis Business Network.

In February 2013, John launched first book Your Elephant's Under Threat which received worldwide acclaim from some of the top business and marketing experts worldwide including: top selling author Brian Tracy, world renowned sales trainer Tom Hopkins, Infusionsoft founder Clate Mask, celebrity branding expert Nick Nanton as well as his own mentor and founder of GKIC, Dan Kennedy.

In May 2014 John won the JCI TOYP (Top Outstanding Young Persons Award) and has been a finalist in the JCI Young Entrepreneur of the year, OMiG marketer of the year and blogging awards.

In April 2015, John launched his second book The Truth! – which hit the top sellers three days in a row and received acclaim from customers and clients the world over. He has also launched numerous training programs, courses both online and offline.

In September 2016, John launched his 3rd book *Direct Response* and in October and November of 2016 he launched two subsequent books *Send in the Wolves* and *The 7 Deadly Sins That Are Crippling Your Business*.

For more information on John and how he can help your business visit www.JohnMulry.com

Also From the Author

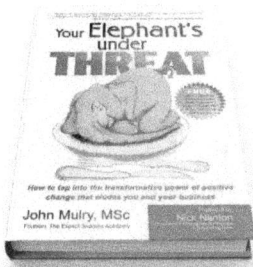

Your Elephant's Under Threat:
John's highly acclaimed first book details his journey from lost, alone, with no direction and living someone else's life to drawing upon the transformative power of positive change within him and the others he surrounded himself with. He changed his life, found happiness, has a business that serves him and now with the information, systems and strategies he shares in this self improvement book, you can too....

Praise for Your Elephant's Under Threat:

"If you're an entrepreneur who's struggling to adapt to the changing world of business or you need a system for defining and getting exactly what you want in life, then you need this book."

- **Brian Tracy International, Legendary Speaker, Trainer and Author of over 60 Best Selling Books**

"The thing about John that most people aren't willing to do, is to actually APPLY the best practices that they learn to their own business and life in order to achieve maximum effectiveness in minimum time. I love the fact that John lives and breathes what he teaches in this book. One of the most important concepts that surfaces in his book is summarized in his three words: INVEST, CONSUME and ACT. If ever there was a simple definition of how to succeed, John has 'nailed it' with these words. Moreover, he's living proof that the invest/consume/act model works."

- **Nick Nanton, CEO of the Dicks + Nanton Celebrity Branding® Agency, Emmy Award Winning Director, Producer & Best-Selling Author**

"In order to achieve success in life, you must first expect it, define it, and apply knowledge gained through education and experience. John Mulry's book, Your Elephant's Under Threat, is an excellent tool to use on your journey."
- **Tom Hopkins International, Speaker and Author of How to Master the Art of Selling**

"What a fantastic, straightforward, and honest book backed by a WONDERFUL story of positive change. If you are an ambitious entrepreneur and want to have your own story of personal triumph and business success, read this book!"

- **Clate Mask, CEO and Co-Founder of InfusionSoft**

"John Mulry's personal story and journey is provocative and profound...He has revealed a lot about personal and business transformation, making it an organised process rather than an accidental evolution."

- **Dan Kennedy, Author & Marketing/Business Strategist**

To get your copy visit <u>www.JohnMulry.com/elephant</u>

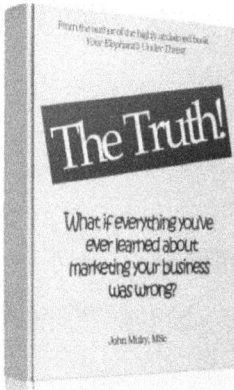

The Truth!

This is more than a book advertising and marketing from one of the leading trusted marketing advisors of our time. It is a book by a man who helps successful businesses become more successful.

It is a bible of tested techniques for anyone interested in creating profitable advertising and marketing – based on empirical evidence from over 200 industries.

And it's one of the most exciting business books you'll ever read.

From John:

"The Truth! isn't just a book, it's a step by step system for marketing your business. It's the book that I wish I had when I first started my business. What I've put together isn't tactics or tricks to work now and then, or it isn't based on one particular media like social media or whatever, it's based on the unchanging principles of human psychology and how people make buying decisions.

I've put it together to be more of a blueprint than just a series of chapters, each one build upon the previous and the end result is a system you'll be able to deploy in your business for attracting your ideal customers."

Praise for The Truth!

"It didn't take long for John's marketing gems to click on a few light bulbs for me and set me straight, as I put together my new advertising campaigns."
-   **Doreen Mellor**

"My mind was blown away by the in-depth business concepts, strategies, tactics, tools and honesty I saw. Before I met you I didn't have a easy to follow and implement system"
-   **Frederick Chelogram**

"At last someone has made an easy actionable blueprint for success, in any niche, without all the fluff and BS. John has made it fail proof not to succeed in business, but only if you get off your butt and put in the action."
-   **Kevin Long**

*"Really helpful, broke everything down into simple to understand, bite sized chunks that helped me get over the fear of marketing."***Pol Murray**

To get you copy of The Truth! Visit www.wrong.ie

www.ingramcontent.com/pod-product-compliance
Lightning Source LLC
Chambersburg PA
CBHW020157200326
41521CB00006B/410